C000319129

HISTORY OF THE IRISH SETTER

As early as the 15th century, dogs called "setters" located game for hunters armed with nets. Those early "setters" looked more like tall spaniels than the setter breeds we recognize today. The Modder Rhu (Gaelic for red spaniel), one probable antecedent of the Irish Setter, was widespread in Ireland during the late 1700s, although its popularity waned as the developing red setter became the dog of the day.

"Big Red," as the Irish Setter is affectionately called, most likely originated in the 1700s from a combination of English Setter, Pointer, various spaniels, a bit of Gordon Setter and perhaps a touch of Irish Water Spaniel. There are no written records of the rollicking red setter's earliest ancestors, as few breeders bothered to jot down pedigrees back then. What mattered in those days was not who a dog's parents were, but how well the

The Irish Setter was developed in Ireland around the beginning of the 18th century. There are no written records of the exact ancestors of this breed.

PHOTO BY ISABELLE FRANCAIS

PHOTO BY ISABELLE FRANCAIS.

English, Irish and Gordon Setters. By the beginning of the 19th century, the Irish Setter was well established. Some parts of Ireland preferred a red-and-white patched dog because it was easier to see when it was hunting.

dog did its job. Before upland bird hunters carried shotguns, their dogs' job was to find game birds and crouch down near them without spooking them into flight. This was called "setting" the game and is where the name "setter" came from. When the dogs were immobile the hunter moved in, throwing a net over both birds and dogs. We can only surmise that the Irish Setter evolved slowly, through selective breeding, as one hunter bred his best "setting" dog to another hunter's finest "setter." Later, when hunters started using firearms, the setter's job description changed slightly. Hunters still wanted their dogs to find and hold game, but now setters were required to point to game in an upright position, the same as the other pointing breeds.

By the beginning of the 1800s, Ireland's setter was well established and recognizable as a specific type of dog, even though early setters were far from identical. Three regions in Ireland preferred three different colors. The south and west favored red-and-white patched setters, explaining that they were easiest to see in the field. The northwest coast was proud of their flashy speckled setters; red dogs with a pattern of small white spots, much like snowflakes, throughout their coats. The solid red setter was developed in northern Ireland and described as a self-red. Its brilliant coat caused much debate. Some hunters rejected the self-colored dogs as too hard to see in the field. Hunters who

America, and it is the Irish Setter recognized by the American Kennel Club.

As showy as the Irish Setter is today, it seems fitting that it was one of the first breeds ever exhibited at a dog show. That show took place in the Town Hall

The setter from Ireland called the Irish Red and White Setter is a separate breed from the Irish Setter, though they are often confused by novices.

preferred them argued that the coat acted as camouflage, enabling the dog to get closer to game birds without being seen. Today, the Irish Red and White Setter is a separate breed on the Emerald Isle and a few sportsmen in the United States also use them for hunting or field trialing. But Ireland's self-colored setter is by far the most popular in

at Newcastle-on-Tyne in England in June of 1859 and was held in conjunction with a poultry show. The only dogs allowed to compete were setters and pointers, and there were 60 entries. Dogs that were entered as the same breed often looked quite different from each other at the earliest dog shows, but competition eventually led to standardization as breeders began to select the most attractive animals as breeding stock.

One of the most influential Irish Setters in breed history was a dog named Palmerston. Bred by Cecil Moore of County Tyrone, Palmerston was whelped around 1870 but wasn't appreciated until years later. Moore kept setters for hunting and believed that 64-pound Palmerston was too lightly built for the field even though the dog was a diligent hunter. When the dog was five years old, Moore took him to a show and offered him for sale for five pounds. No one bought Palmerston, so Moore told his kennel man to drown him because he didn't feel the dog should be used for breeding. Instead, the kennel man sold or gave the dog to a show dog fancier named T. M. Hilliard. According to popular history, Hilliard wasn't too excited about Palmerston either, but decided to give him a try at the dog shows. It was the beginning of a legend. Palmerston had such an extraordinary career as a show dog that a judge bought part interest in him. Soon Palmerston was the most popular stud dog in the country, siring hundreds of puppies. Even the thin white stripe on his forehead became a type of trademark as every Irish Setter fancier wanted to own a dog with the "Palmerston snip."

PHOTO BY ISABELLE FRANCAIS.

The Irish Setter was an early entry in livestock shows. In 1859, in Newcastle-on-Tyne (England), with only setters and pointers allowed in the show, 60 dogs showed up to compete.

PHOTO BY ISABELLE FRANCAIS.

Irish Setters have not lost their charm as people-lovers and Irish people themselves used their considerable charm to promote this export from the Emerald Isle.

Palmerston had a profound influence on the development of the Irish Setter breed. When he died in 1880, his head was mounted and shipped to America where it graced the Waldorf-Astoria Hotel in New York City, which was managed by Hilliard's son. It became the property of the Irish Setter Club of America in 1918.

THE IRISH SETTER IN AMERICA

In 1875, while Palmerston was making a name for himself on the Emerald Isle, a dog named Elcho, imported from Ireland and owned by the St. Louis Kennel Club, became the ambassador for the breed in the United States. He was the first Irish Setter to become an American bench show champion and won awards at shows in major cities throughout the East and Midwest. He also sired 197 puppies from 51 different dams, and an amazing number of them became successful show dogs and field trial winners. In 1877, Ch. Elcho became the private hunting dog of Dr. William Jarvis of Claremont, New Hampshire. Jarvis also owned Irish imports Rose and Noreen, a daughter and a granddaughter of Palmerston. Several breedings of Rose and Noreen to Ch. Elcho produced excellent foundation stock, getting the Irish Setter off to a secure start in America.

It wasn't long before the rakish red setter became popular in America, and many fine dogs were imported from Ireland and bred in the United States. Prices soared, but people were willing to pay for a spectacular specimen and many

The green of Ireland with the red hair which typifies Irish beauties makes the Irish Setter one of the world's most beautiful dogs. Add a rakish personality and you can buy a piece of Ireland that barks!

PHOTO BY ISABELLE FRANCAIS.

considered the Irish Setter the most beautiful of all breeds. By the end of World War I, it was the darling of celebrities, and film stars Mary Pickford and Janet Gaynor both publicly adored their Irish Setters. The combination of beauty and popularity proved to be both a blessing and a curse. Soon Irish Setters were bred for their good looks without regard for their working ability and became the breed of choice of dog show exhibitors and fashionable pet owners. Few red setters had the opportunity to demonstrate their prowess in field trials, or even as hunting companions. Eventually several strains of Irish Setters lost the instincts necessary to be useful in the field, but no one seemed to notice or care.

Popularity also resulted in over-breeding. People who bred dogs purely for profit jumped on the Irish Setter bandwagon, mating inferior animals and selling the high-strung, often skitterish puppies for big bucks. When enough of these sad specimens were circulated throughout the country, the breed's popularity waned. Then the profiteers moved on to other breeds and the honest, reputable Irish Setter breeders took over again. Eventually they repaired most of the damage, and once again produced strikingly beautiful dogs with healthy bodies and stable temperaments.

Today, thanks to the efforts of the Irish Setter Club of America, many of the strains that produced show and pet dogs for generations are able to add hunting ability to their list of attributes. The club has a Dual Dog Committee, charged with promoting and recognizing Irish Setters that earn championships in both the show ring and the field. During the past 20 years, over 200 Irish Setters have won American Kennel Club

The Irish Setter standard calls for a mahogany or rich, chestnut red coat with no black. A small amount of white on the chest, as shown here, is not to be penalized.

PHOTO BY ISABELLE FRANCAIS.

(AKC) Field Championships, and according to the Irish Setter Club of America's Centennial Edition Pictorial, the breed now boasts 16 dual champions. The impressive Irishman, still a top-winning show dog and a cherished companion, is apparently on the comeback trail as a hunting companion.

STANDARD FOR THE IRISH SETTER

General Appearance—The Irish Setter is an active, aristocratic bird dog, rich red in color, substantial yet elegant in build. Standing over two feet tall at the shoulder, the dog has a straight, fine, glossy coat, longer on ears, chest, tail and back of legs. Afield, the Irish Setter is a swift-moving balance, whether standing or in motion. Each part of the dog flows and fits smoothly into its neighboring parts without calling attention to itself.

Size, Proportion, Substance—There is no disqualification as to size. The make and fit of all parts and their overall balance in the

PHOTO BY ISABELLE FRANCAIS.

The Irish Setter should be over two feet tall with a fine, glossy coat which is longer on its ears, chest, tail and the back of its legs.

hunter; at home, a sweet natured, trainable companion.

At their best, the lines of the Irish Setter so satisfy in overall balance that artist have termed it the most beautiful of all dogs. The correct specimen always exhibits animal are rated more important. 27 inches at the withers and a show weight of about 70 pounds is considered ideal for the dog; the bitch 25 inches, 60 pounds. Variance beyond an inch up or down is to be discouraged.

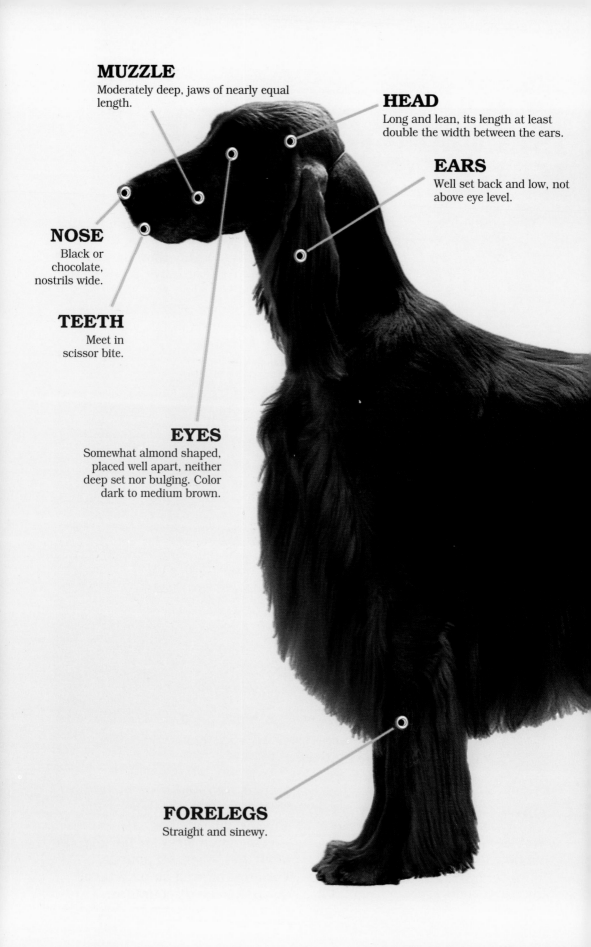

MUZZLE
Moderately deep, jaws of nearly equal length.

HEAD
Long and lean, its length at least double the width between the ears.

EARS
Well set back and low, not above eye level.

NOSE
Black or chocolate, nostrils wide.

TEETH
Meet in scissor bite.

EYES
Somewhat almond shaped, placed well apart, neither deep set nor bulging. Color dark to medium brown.

FORELEGS
Straight and sinewy.

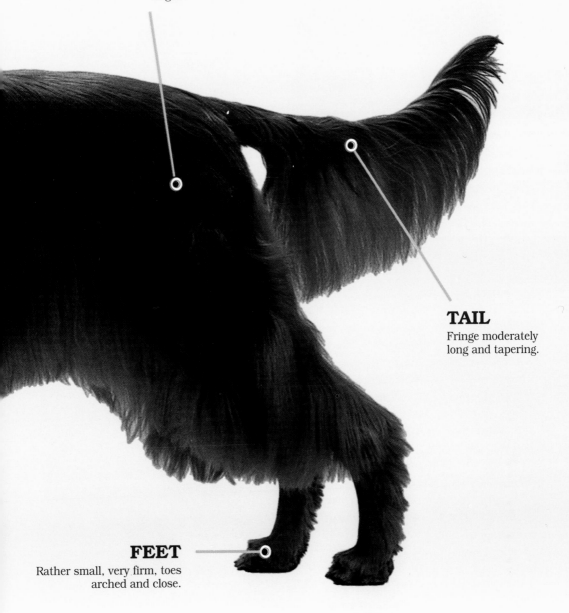

The ideal Irish Setter as portrayed by Ch. Pin Oak Vicksburg, Best of Breed at the 1996 Westminster Kennel Club Show. Owned by Pam Krothe, Timmy and Nancy Godbey.

PHOTO BY ISABELLE FRANCAIS.

HINDQUARTERS
de and powerful with well developed thighs.

TAIL
Fringe moderately long and tapering.

FEET
Rather small, very firm, toes arched and close.

PHOTO BY ISABELLE FRANCAIS.

The proportion of the Irish Setter must be such that it is slightly longer (without the head) than it is tall.

Proportion—Measuring from the breastbone to the rear of the thigh and from the top of the withers to the ground, the Irish Setter is slightly longer than it is tall. *Substance*—All legs sturdy with plenty of bone. Structure in the male reflects masculinity without coarseness. Bitches appear feminine without being slight of bone.

Head—Long and lean, its length at least double the width between the ears. Beauty of head is emphasized by delicate chiseling along the muzzle, around and below the eyes, and along the cheeks. *Expression* soft, yet alert. *Eyes* somewhat almond shaped, of medium size, placed rather well apart, neither deep set nor bulging. Color, dark to medium brown. *Ears* set well back and low, not above level of the eye. Leather thin, hanging in a neat fold close to the head, and nearly long enough to reach the nose. The *skull* is oval when viewed

from above or front; very slightly domed when viewed in profile. The brow is raised, showing a distinct stop midway between the tip of the nose and the well-defined occiput (rear point of skull). Thus the nearly level line from occiput to brow is set a little above, and parallel to, the straight and equal line from eye to nose. *Muzzle* moderately deep, jaws of nearly equal length, the underline of the jaws being almost parallel with the top line of the muzzle. *Nose* black or chocolate; nostrils wide. Upper lips fairly square but not pendulous. The *teeth* meet in a scissors bite in which the upper incisors fit closely over the lower, or they may meet evenly.

Neck, Topline, Body—*Neck* moderately long, strong but not thick, and slightly arched; free from throatiness and fitting smoothly into the shoulders. *Topline* of body from withers to tail should be firm and incline

This Irish Setter puppy may look like its neck is too long, but the moderately long thin neck is a desirable trait.

PHOTO BY ISABELLE FRANCAIS.

slightly downward without sharp drop at the croup. The *tail* is set on nearly level with the croup as a natural extension of the topline, strong at root, tapering to a fine point, nearly long enough to reach the hock. Carriage straight or curving slightly upward, nearly level with the back. *Body* sufficiently long to permit a straight and free stride. *Chest* deep, reaching approximately to the elbows, with moderate forechest, extending beyond the point where the shoulder joins the upper arm. Chest is of moderate width so that it does not interfere with forward motion and extends rearwards to well sprung ribs. *Loins* firm, muscular and of moderate length.

Forequarters— Shoulder blades long, wide, sloping well back, fairly close together at the withers. Upper arm and shoulder blades are approximately the same length, and are joined at sufficient angle to bring the elbows rearward along the brisket in line with the top of the withers. The elbows moving freely, incline neither in nor out. *Forelegs* straight and sinewy. Strong, nearly straight pastern. *Feet* rather small, very firm, toes arched and close.

Hindquarters—Hindquarters should be wide and powerful with broad, well-developed thighs. Hind legs long and muscular from hip to hock; short and perpendicular from hock to ground; well angulated at stifle and hock joints, which, like the elbows, incline neither in nor out. Feet as in front. Angulation of the forequarters and hindquarters should be balanced.

Coat—Short and fine on head and forelegs. On all other parts of moderate length and flat. Feathering long and silky on ears; on back of forelegs and thighs long and fine, with a pleasing fringe of hair on belly and brisket extending onto the chest. Fringe on tail moderately long and tapering. All coat and feathering as straight as possible from curl or wave. The Irish Setter is trimmed for the show ring to emphasize the lean head and

PHOTO BY ISABELLE FRANCAIS.

The head of a good Irish Setter should be long and lean with a length at least double the width between the ears. It should have a soft, yet alert, facial expression.

PHOTO BY ISABELLE FRANCAIS.

The way an Irish Setter moves is important. The gait during trotting is big and very lively, graceful and efficient. At an extended trot, the head reaches forward to keep the dog in balance.

clean neck. The top third of the ears and the throat nearly to the breastbone are trimmed. Excess feathering is removed to show the natural outline of the foot. All trimming is done to preserve the natural appearance of the dog.

Color—Mahogany or rich chestnut red with no black. A small amount of white on chest, throat or toes, or a narrow centered streak on skull is not to be penalized.

Gait—At the trot the gait is big, very lively, graceful and efficient. At an extended trot the head reaches forward, keeping the dog in balance. The forelegs reach well ahead as if to pull in the ground without giving the appearance of a hackney gait. The hindquarters drive smoothly and with great power. Seen from the front or the rear, the forelegs, as well as the hind legs below the hock joint, move perpendicularly to the round, with some tendency towards a single track as speed increases. Structural characteristics which interfere with a straight, true stride are to be penalized.

Temperament—The Irish Setter has a rollicking personality. Shyness, hostility or timidity are uncharacteristic of the breed. An outgoing, stable temperament is the essence of the Irish Setter.

Approved August 14, 1990
Effective September 30, 1990

CHARACTERISTICS OF THE IRISH SETTER

A big, rollicking dog with a uniquely rich red coat, the Irish Setter embodies a complex combination of intriguing opposites. In appearance, it is sturdy and substantial, but also the epitome of elegance. The breed stands tall (27" at the withers for a male and 25" for a female), and sports a smooth and beautifully balanced outline set off by a long, lean and delicately chiseled head, dark, almond-shaped eyes and an alert but soft expression. His mahogany or deep chestnut red coat is short and fine on the head and forelegs and of medium length on the body. The feathering on the ears, tail, back of the forelegs and back of the thighs is long, silky and straight, with an appealing fringe on the chest, extending backward through the brisket and belly.

Aristocratic in appearance, but not necessarily in behavior, more Irish Setters act the part of the court jester rather than of the

The coat of the Irish Setter should be short and fine on the head and forelegs. It should be of moderate length and flat on other parts of the body. In all cases it should be flat and not curly.

PHOTO BY ISABELLE FRANCAIS.

PHOTO BY ISABELLE FRANCAIS.

Irish Setters are hunting dogs by nature and are at their happiest when used in the field or for some other purposeful activity.

king, especially when they are young. Originally bred to be bird dogs, they are intelligent, independent thinkers with a high activity level — attributes which make for either a fabulous combination or a fiasco, depending on the owner. The breed's quick intelligence and desire for action is bound to be a problem if you leave your dog to his own devices. The same qualities that make these dogs so compelling — spirit, energy, a strong sense of humor and an active brain — can turn a neglected or untrained Irish Setter into a wily rogue. The Irish Setter is happiest and behaves the best when he has a sense of purpose. When widely used as a hunting dog, he enjoyed the dual benefits of a challenging job and plenty of exercise, and he returned home relaxed, fulfilled and well-behaved. Few modern-day Irish Setters have the opportunity to do the work they were originally bred for, but with training, exercise and a sense of purpose they still become charming companions. Check the newspaper classifieds or ask your veterinarian where there is a puppy kindergarten, obedience or agility school near you. Training your Irish Setter will be an ongoing avocation and should be started early for best results.

The Irish Setter develops slowly—physically, mentally and emotionally—so don't be disappointed if your clumsy red pup isn't the star of the beginners

The Irish Setter develops slowly. Don't be discouraged—patience and persistence are the keys to a successfully trained dog.

PHOTO BY KAREN TAYLOR.

obedience or agility class. The breed loves to please but lacks adult coordination until he is nearly two years old and may not develop his mature attention span until he is pushing three years of age. Consequently, you may find yourself with the largest, but most contradictions in the Irish Setter's makeup is that under the happy-go-lucky attitude lurks a sensitive spirit. Don't crush it, and your flaming red dog will eventually learn to work with flamboyance and joy. Best of all, he will continue working happily all his

PHOTO BY ISABELLE FRANCAIS.

The Irishmen are happy-go-lucky dogs. They love human companionship and are slow to take orders from anyone—constant training is necessary for a successful human/dog relationship.

puppyish, dog in the class. Patience and persistence are the keys to successfully training the jovial Irishman. Be calm and consistent in your corrections and never, ever lose your temper. Physically punishing or loudly berating your Irish Setter simply won't work. In fact, it could do irreparable harm to your dog's working attitude. One of the life. The Irish Setter is a stayer. He's there for the long haul. It may take him a while to grow up and settle down, but once he learns something, he never forgets. Do without a dog if you don't have time to give one the vital gift of basic training. All dogs are social animals that need guidance and companionship. There are many other types of

PHOTO BY ISABELLE FRANCAIS.

Although the American Kennel Club classifies the Irish Setter as a sporting breed, he can be a warm, friendly family dog if he has been properly socialized.

pets available that readily adapt to long hours of solitude.

Socialization brings out the best in an Irish Setter's personality. It means familiarizing a puppy (or new dog) with the people, animals, objects and noises it may encounter during everyday life. Vaccinated puppies should be introduced to friendly people of all ages and both sexes, and to non-menacing, well-mannered dogs. They should ride in cars other than for trips to the veterinarian; walk on varied footing, such as linoleum, concrete, grass, wood and carpet; and encounter bicycles, shopping carts, joggers, people in wheelchairs and traffic sounds — all while on lead, of course. Always be cautious for your puppy as he may approach adult dogs and use canine body language, such as play-bowing, to invite them to romp. While most dogs recognize a puppy's good will instantly and eagerly join in the fun, not every mature dog will be in the mood to play.

The Irish Setter is classified by the American Kennel Club as a Sporting breed — another word for hunting dog. And that's exactly what Big Red was a century ago, and, with training and opportunity, often is today. Built to cover many miles quickly and bold enough to tackle the toughest terrain, a well-conditioned Irish Setter can hunt for hours without tiring. Staying power, enthusiasm and a high activity level were built into sporting dogs as these attributes went hand in hand with hunting instinct. While not every Irish Setter retains a strong hunting instinct, most modern sporting dogs still have dogs in a nearby park. When too closely confined, a bored Irishman may become hyperactive or even destructive. He needs play time and enough space to stretch out and run. Irish Setters do fine in family homes with fenced-in yards, even if the yards aren't especially large. The typical Irishman adores children, and will happily play games with them for

PHOTO BY ISABELLE FRANCAIS.

Passed from generation to generation, the Irish Setter still retains his strong hunting instinct and love for the outdoors, and will thrive if given plenty of play and exercise.

the other three attributes. In addition to training, they need exercise — and plenty of it. Consequently, the Irish Setter isn't a good choice for an apartment dog unless you jog a few miles daily and take your dog along, or live in a city that provides an enclosed play area for hours provided the youngsters have been taught how to handle a pet with love and respect. While the Irish Setter is sturdy enough to enjoy some rough and tumble, young children should enjoy their pet with adult supervision until they are old enough to understand that dogs have

PHOTO BY ROBERT PEARCY.

A typical Irish Setter loves people and is a superb family dog. Remember that they are not small dogs and they should always be handled with care and respect.

intelligence and feelings, and are not battery-operated toys fit for pulling and poking.

While some Irish Setters are alert watchdogs, barking a loud warning when a stranger heads for the door, others absolutely adore the whole human race and happily greet all who come to the door. If you are looking for a big guard dog, the Irishman isn't it, although his size alone will keep all but the boldest burglars away.

Living with Big Red is never boring. An exceptionally beautiful animal, he moves with lively grace, attracting admiring attention wherever he goes. Spirited and sweet-natured, loving and loyal, this breed greets each day with renewed cheer. The Irish Setter loves human companionship and will contentedly curl up beside your chair and gaze up at you adoringly. He delights in being scratched behind the ears and may poke his head up under your hand or rest his head on your knee as an unsubtle reminder. Regal, yet comical, with a well-developed sense of fun, your devil-may-care Irishman will play at the slightest provocation and retain its puppyish love of toys and games into old age. When matched with the right owner, the Irish Setter is intelligent, versatile and content, exuding endless charm and a love of life that can be contagious.

PHOTO BY ISABELLE FRANCAIS.

Selecting an Irish Setter puppy is one of life's more important projects. The Big Red will live with you for a long time and become one of your most trusted and pleasurable companions. Take your time and make your choice carefully.

YOUR NEW IRISH SETTER PUPPY

SELECTION

When you do pick out a Irish Setter puppy as a pet, don't be hasty; the longer you study puppies, the better you will understand them. Make it your transcendent concern to select only one that radiates good health retreat to his bed or his box, or plays coy behind other puppies or people, or hides his head under your arm or jacket appealing to your protective instinct. *Pick the Irish Setter puppy who forthrightly picks you! The feeling of attraction should be mutual!*

PHOTO BY ISABELLE FRANCAIS.

Pick the Irish Setter puppy that picks you! There should be a mutual attraction, but don't expect this attraction to be instantaneous. You should handle the whole litter before deciding on *the* puppy for you.

and spirit and is lively on his feet, whose eyes are bright, whose coat shines, and who comes forward eagerly to make and to cultivate your acquaintance. Don't fall for any shy little darling that wants to

DOCUMENTS

Now, a little paper work is in order. When you purchase a purebred Irish Setter puppy, you should receive a transfer of ownership, registration material, and other "papers" (a list of the

PHOTO BY ISABELLE FRANCAIS.

How do you choose just one? You will spend a lot of time choosing the right Irish Setter puppy, so don't rush the final decision.

immunization shots, if any, the puppy may have been given; a note on whether or not the puppy has been wormed; a diet and feeding schedule to which the puppy is accustomed) and you are welcomed as a fellow owner to a long, pleasant association with a most lovable pet, and more (news)paper work.

GENERAL PREPARATION

You have chosen to own a particular Irish Setter puppy. You have chosen it very carefully over all other breeds and all other puppies. So before you ever get that Irish Setter puppy home, you will have prepared for its arrival by reading everything you can get your hands on having to do with the management of Irish Setters

and puppies. True, you will run into many conflicting opinions, but at least you will not be starting "blind." Read, study, digest. Talk over your plans with your veterinarian, other "Irish Setter people," and the seller of your Irish Setter puppy.

When you get your Irish Setter puppy, you will find that your reading and study are far from finished. You've just scratched the surface in your plan to provide the greatest possible comfort and health for your Irish Setter; and, by the same token, you do want to assure yourself of the greatest possible enjoyment of this wonderful creature. You must be ready for this puppy mentally as well as in the physical requirements.

TRANSPORTATION

If you take the puppy home by car, protect him from drafts, particularly in cold weather. Wrapped in a towel and carried in the arms or lap of a passenger, the Irish Setter puppy will usually make the trip without mishap. If the pup starts to drool and to squirm, stop the car for a few minutes. Have newspapers handy in case of car-sickness. A covered carton lined with newspapers provides protection for puppy and car, if you are driving alone. Avoid excitement and unnecessary handling of the puppy on arrival. A Irish Setter puppy is a very small "package" to be making a complete change of surroundings and company, and he needs frequent rest and refreshment to renew his vitality.

If possible, see the sire, dam, and littermates of the Irish Setter puppy you are considering so that you have some idea of what your puppy will be like when it matures.

PHOTO BY VINCE SERBIN.

If you are going to pick up your Irish Setter puppy, purchase a proper crate. He'll need it for housebreaking and training, too.

THE FIRST DAY AND NIGHT

When your Irish Setter puppy arrives in your home, put him down on the floor and don't pick him up again, except when it is absolutely necessary. He is a dog, a real dog, and must not be lugged around like a rag doll. Handle him as little as possible, and permit no one to pick him up and baby him. To repeat, *put your Irish Setter puppy on the floor or the ground and let him stay there except when it may be necessary to do otherwise.*

Quite possibly your Irish Setter puppy will be afraid for a while in his new surroundings, without his mother and littermates. Comfort him and reassure him, but don't console him. Don't give him the "oh-you-poor-itsy-bitsy-puppy" treatment. Be calm, friendly, and reassuring. Encourage him to walk around and sniff over his new home. If it's dark, put on the lights. Let him roam for a few minutes while you and everyone else concerned sit quietly or go about your routine business. Let the puppy come back to you.

Playmates may cause an immediate problem if the new Irish Setter puppy is to be greeted by children or other pets. If not, you can skip this subject. The natural affinity between puppies and children calls for some supervision until a live-and-let-live relationship is established. This applies particularly to a Christmas puppy, when there is more excitement than usual and more chance for a puppy to swallow something upsetting. It is a better plan to welcome the puppy several days before or after the holiday week. Like a baby, your Irish Setter puppy needs much rest and should not be over-handled. Once a child realizes that a puppy has "feelings"

similar to his own, and can readily be hurt or injured, the opportunities for play and responsibilities provide exercise and training for both.

For his first night with you, he should be put where he is to sleep every night—say in the kitchen, since its floor can usually be easily cleaned. Let him explore the kitchen to his heart's content; close doors to confine him there. Prepare his food and feed him lightly the first night. Give him a pan with some water in it—not a lot, since most puppies will try to drink the whole pan dry. Give him an old coat or shirt to lie on. Since a coat or shirt will be strong in human scent, he will pick it out to lie on, thus furthering his feeling of security in the room where he has just been fed.

PHOTO BY VINCE SERBIN.

When you take your new puppy home, he may miss the company of his dam and littermates. Pay extra attention to him during this lonely time.

PHOTO BY ISABELLE FRANCAIS.

Irish Setter puppies are sweet, adorable and loving, but, unless they are trained, all of these delightful characteristics fade when the puppy makes a puddle on your floor (hopefully not on a rug!). Simply stated, *your puppy must be housebroken.*

HOUSEBREAKING HELPS

Now, sooner or later—mostly sooner—your new Irish Setter puppy is going to "puddle" on the floor. First take a newspaper and lay it on the puddle until the urine is soaked up onto the paper. *Save this paper.* Now take a cloth with soap and water, wipe up the floor and dry it well. Then take the wet paper and place it on a fairly large square of newspapers in a convenient corner. When cleaning up, always keep a piece of wet paper on top of the others. Every time he wants to "squat," he will seek out this spot and use the papers. (This routine is rarely necessary for more than three days.) Now leave your Irish Setter puppy for the night. Quite probably he will cry and howl a bit; some are more stubborn than others on this matter. But let him stay alone for the night. This may seem harsh treatment, but it is the best procedure in the long run. Just let him cry; he will weary of it sooner or later.

TRAINING

You owe proper training to your Irish Setter. The right and privilege of being trained is his birthright; and whether your Irish Setter is going to be a handsome, well-mannered housedog and companion, a show dog, or whatever possible use he may be put to, the basic training is always the same—all must start with basic obedience, or what might be called "manner training."

Your Irish Setter must come instantly when called and obey the "Sit" or "Down" command just as fast; he must walk quietly at "Heel," whether on or off lead. He must be mannerly and polite wherever he goes; he must be polite to strangers on the street and in stores. He must be mannerly in the presence of other dogs. He must not bark at children on roller skates, motorcycles, or other domestic animals. And he must be restrained from chasing cats. It is not a dog's inalienable right to chase cats, and he must be reprimanded for it.

Educating an active breed like the Irish Setter is vital. Basic training creates a close bond between dog and owner.

PHOTO BY VINCE SERBIN.

PHOTO BY VINCE SERBIN.

PHOTO BY VINCE SERBIN.

"Down" is the most natural position of a dog.

"Sit/stay" is an important command should your puppy start chasing another dog or cat into the street.

Making and maintaining eye contact is an important characteristic of dog training.

Your Irish Setter must obey all commands, whether from you or from your children.

PHOTO BY VINCE SERBIN.

PHOTO BY ISABELLE FRANCAIS.

If your youngster is going to spend a lot of time with your Irish Setter, the child must be taught how to train and discipline the puppy.

PHOTO BY ISABELLE FRANCAIS.

PROFESSIONAL TRAINING

How do you go about this training? Well, it's a very simple procedure, pretty well standardized by now. First, if you can afford the extra expense, you may send your Irish Setter to a professional trainer, where in 30 you will have to go for some training, too, after the trainer feels your Irish Setter is ready to go home. You will have to learn how your Irish Setter works, just what to expect of him and how to use what the dog has learned after he is home.

Kids must take responsibility for the safety, care and comfort of their pet puppy. Teach them to participate in all aspects of their Irish Setter's training and care.

to 60 days he will learn how to be a "good dog." If you enlist the services of a good professional trainer, follow his advice of when to come to see the dog. No, he won't forget you, but too-frequent visits at the wrong time may slow down his training progress. And using a "pro" trainer means that

OBEDIENCE TRAINING CLASS

Another way to train your Irish Setter (many experienced Irish Setter people think this is the best) is to join an obedience training class right in your own community. There is such a group in nearly every community nowadays. Here you will be working with a group of people who are also just starting out. You will actually be training your own dog, since all work is done under the direction of a head trainer who will make suggestions to you and also tell you when and how to correct your Irish Setter's errors. Then, too, working with such a group, your Irish Setter will learn to get along with other dogs. And, what is more important, he will learn to do exactly what he is told to do, no matter how much confusion there is around him or how great the temptation is to go his own way.

Write to your national kennel club for the location of a training club or class in your locality. Sign up. Go to it regularly—every session! Go early and leave late! Both you and your Irish Setter will benefit tremendously.

If you have been the Irish Setter's trainer, then you must introduce him to the other members of the family by having them handle the dog in your presence.

SUCCESSFUL DOG TRAINING
TS-205

**TRAINING YOUR DOG FOR SPORTS
AND OTHER ACTIVITIES - TS-258**

TRAIN HIM BY THE BOOK

The third way of training your Irish Setter is by the book. Yes, you can do it this way and do a good job of it too. But in using the book method, select a book, buy it, study it carefully; then study it some more, until the procedures are almost second nature to you. Then start your training. But stay with the book and its advice and exercises. Don't start in and then make up a few rules of your own. If you don't follow the book, you'll get into jams you can't get out of by yourself. If after a few hours of short training sessions your Irish Setter is still not working as he should, get back to the book for a study session, because it's your fault, not the dog's! The procedures of dog training have been so well systemized that it must be your fault, since literally thousands of fine Irish Setters have been trained by the book.

After your Irish Setter is "letter perfect" under all conditions, then, if you wish, go on to advanced training and trick work.

Your Irish Setter will love his obedience training, and you'll burst with pride at the finished product! Your Irish Setter will enjoy life even more, and you'll enjoy your Irish Setter more. And remember—you *owe good training to your Irish Setter.*

**BECOMING YOUR DOG'S BEST FRIEND.
TS-220**

A great advantage of training your Irish Setter is that he will stand still for grooming.

PHOTO BY ROBERT PEARCY.

SHOWING YOUR IRISH SETTER

A show Irish Setter is a comparatively rare thing. He is one out of several litters of puppies. He happens to be born with a degree of physical perfection that closely approximates the standard by which the breed is judged in the show ring. Such a dog should, on maturity, be able to win or approach his championship in good, fast company at the larger shows. Upon finishing his championship, he is apt to be as highly desirable as a breeding animal. As a proven stud, he will automatically command a high price for service.

Showing Irish Setters is a lot of fun—yes, but it is a highly competitive sport. While all the experts were once beginners, the odds are against a novice. You will be showing against experienced handlers, often people who have devoted a lifetime to breeding, picking the right ones, and then showing those dogs through to their championships. Moreover, the most perfect Irish Setter ever born has faults, and in your hands the faults will be far more evident than with the experienced handler who knows how to minimize his Irish Setter's faults. These are but a few points on the sad side of the picture.

An example of beautiful show-quality Irish Setters competing in a Fun Match for young dogs.

The experienced handler, as I say, was not born knowing the ropes. He learned—*and so can you!* You can if you will put in the same time, study and keen observation that he did. But it will take time!

KEY TO SUCCESS

First, search for a truly fine show prospect. Take the puppy home, raise him by the book, and as carefully as you know how, give him every chance to mature into the Irish Setter you hoped for. My advice is to keep your dog out of big shows, even Puppy Classes, until he is mature. Maturity in the male is roughly two years; with the female, 14 months or so. When your Irish Setter is approaching maturity, start out at match shows, and, with this experience for both of you, then go gunning for the big wins at the big shows.

Next step, read the standard by which the Irish Setter is judged. Study it until you know it by heart. Having done this, and while your puppy is at home (where he should be) growing into a normal, healthy Irish Setter, go to every dog show you can possibly reach. Sit at the ringside and watch Irish Setter judging. Keep your ears and eyes open. Do your own judging, holding each of those dogs against the standard, which you now know by heart.

In your evaluations, don't start looking for faults. Look for the

Dogs must usually be penned at open shows; remember these are the same crates used to bring your dog home and in housebreaking.

During the dog show, the owners and handlers are very busy with last-minute details. After the show they'll usually be happy to talk about Irish Setters with you.

virtues—the best qualities. How does a given Irish Setter shape up against the standard? Having looked for and noted the virtues, then note the faults and see what prevents a given Irish Setter from standing correctly or moving well. Weigh these faults against the virtues, since, ideally, every feature of the dog should contribute to the harmonious whole dog.

"RINGSIDE JUDGING"

It's a good practice to make notes on each Irish Setter, always holding the dog against the standard. In "ringside judging," forget your personal preference for this or that feature. What does the standard say about it? Watch carefully as the judge places the dogs in a given class. It is difficult from the ringside always to see why number one was placed over the second dog. Try to follow the judge's reasoning. Later try to talk with the judge after he is finished. Ask him questions as to why he placed certain Irish Setters and not others. Listen while the judge explains his placings, and, I'll say right here, any judge worthy of his license should be able to give reasons.

When you're not at the ringside, talk with the fanciers and breeders who have Irish Setters. Don't be afraid to ask opinions or say that you don't know. You have a lot of listening to do, and it will help you a great deal and speed up your personal progress if you are a good listener.

In conformation, your dog is judged on how closely he conforms to the standard of the breed.

Match shows and dog shows in general are usually a lot of fun. You can get much more enjoyment from your Irish Setter by participating in dog events...and you can meet the nicest people, too!

Besides basic training in obedience, there are many other types of activities that your Irish Setter can master. This Irishman shows his athleticism and versatility by competing in obedience trials.

THE NATIONAL CLUB

You will find it worthwhile to join the national Irish Setter club and to subscribe to its magazine. From the national club, you will learn the location of an approved regional club near you. Now, when your young Irish Setter is eight to ten months old, find out the dates of match shows in your section of the country. These differ from regular shows only in that no championship points are given. These shows are especially designed to launch young dogs (and new handlers) on a show career.

ENTER MATCH SHOWS

With the ring deportment you have watched at big shows firmly in mind and practice, enter your Irish Setter in as many match shows as you can. When in the ring, you have two jobs. One is to see to it that your Irish Setter is always being seen to its best advantage. The other job is to keep your eye on the judge to see what he may want you to do next. Watch only the judge and your Irish Setter. Be quick and be alert; do exactly as the judge directs. Don't speak to him except to answer his questions. If he does something you don't like, don't say so. And don't irritate the judge (and everybody else) by constantly talking and fussing with your dog.

In moving about the ring, remember to keep clear of dogs beside you or in front of you. It is my advice to you *not* to show your Irish Setter in a regular point show until he is at least close to maturity and after both you and your dog have had time to perfect ring manners and poise in the match shows.

YOUR IRISH SETTER'S HEALTH

Richly garbed in vibrant red, your Irish Setter should present a stirring picture of enthusiasm and health. A lively dog with a devil-may-care attitude, the Irish Setter does not feign illness or injury to elicit attention. In fact, your dog is more likely to act as if nothing is wrong, even when something is. Trust your instincts. No one knows your dog better than you, so on the rare occasions when something seems wrong, don't wait to see what will happen. Instead, visit your veterinarian right away. In many cases, prompt treatment is the key to a quick recovery.

SPECIAL CONSIDERATIONS

Leggy, awkward and active, your Irish Setter may be an accident-prone puppy before he becomes a graceful and agile adult. Not only that, but he will be a puppy for a long time. An extremely slow-maturing breed, the Irish Setter isn't physically or mentally mature until nearly three years old, although it seems to become less accident prone after passing the 18-month mark.

An occasional Irish Setter puppy suffers a growth disturbance. One of the most common problems associated with growth in many large breeds is hypertrophic osteodystrophy (HOD), a disease of unknown origin that makes bones and joints painful and swollen. Puppies often outgrow HOD but may be left with bone deformities of varying severity. In recent years, oversupplementation (too many vitamin or mineral additives or just plain overfeeding) has been suspected as being either a cause of HOD or a contributing factor. Another growth disorder, osteochondritis dessicans (OCD) may be inherited, but is probably also caused or aggravated by nutritional factors. It induces joint pain and lameness, and may damage or kill the cartilage. To lessen the chances of your Irish Setter puppy coming down with HOD or OCD, resist the urge to give him vitamins or minerals, and if your veterinarian prescribes a nutritional supplement, give it exactly according to directions. When working with nutritional balances, if a little of something is good, a lot isn't better. In fact, a lot could be downright dangerous.

Hip dysplasia, a deformity of the hip joint that varies in severity from mild to crippling, affects approximately one-third of all Irish Setters — a percentage that is equal to or less than many other large breeds and seems to be on the decrease. Believed to have a genetic background, it can also be aggravated by oversupplementation or overfeeding. Raising a healthy Irish Setter is not an avocation for the impatient. While it's tempting to encourage a gawky adolescent to eat more food than he needs so

Irish Setters are very slow to mature. The typical Irish Setter will not be physically or mentally mature until nearly three years of age.

PHOTO BY VINCE SERBIN.

he fills out quickly, too much substance strains young joints and puts undue pressure on unsolidified bones, causing potential long-term problems.

Eye disorders common to many breeds show up occasionally in the Irish Setter. Among these problems are progressive retinal atrophy (PRA), an inherited degeneration of the retina that eventually leads to blindness; entropion, a condition characterized by the eyelids rolling inward, causing the hair to rub on the cornea and leading to irritation and possibly visual losses from scarring; and ectropion, a problem characterized by red, inflamed eyes and caused by the lower eyelids hanging loosely and accumulating irritants. Some older Irish Setters get cataracts, and an occasional unlucky younger dog suffers from juvenile cataracts.

Frequent vomiting should not be taken lightly in an Irish Setter. It could indicate persistent right aortic arch, an abnormal artery that constricts the esophagus and can only be corrected by surgery.

To acquire a healthy, trainable Irish Setter with a sound temperament, purchase your puppy from a reputable breeder. Chances are you'll have a beautiful, spirited and intelligent companion for many years. If you do the choosing, remember that the best puppies play happily with their littermates, are glad to meet

You should examine your Irish Setter carefully and frequently to be aware of any physical or medical problems as early as possible.

PHOTO BY ISABELLE FRANCAIS.

Keep your Irish Setter puppy away from other dogs until their *permanent shots* have been administered. Be careful...many shots are only *permanent* for one year!

you and are neither the bully nor the "scaredy-cat" of the litter. Choose a happy-go-lucky youngster with clear skin, bright eyes and a shiny coat.

Your new Irish Setter should visit the veterinarian for a thorough examination within 48 hours after you acquire him. The veterinarian will set up his vaccination schedule and rid him of parasites.

VACCINATIONS

Many of the most dangerous canine diseases are preventable through vaccinations, while other problems can be avoided through good nutrition and dependable daily care. Keep your puppy away from crowds of people and strange

dogs until his inoculations are complete. The final puppy vaccinations are often referred to as "permanent shots," but they are only "permanent" for a year. Following his puppy series, your Irish Setter will need booster vaccinations every year of his adult life. These vaccines protect your dog from diseases such as distemper, hepatitis, leptospirosis, parvovirus, parainfluenza, tracheobronchitis, coronavirus, Lyme disease and rabies.

Distemper, an airborne virus, is the number one killer of unvaccinated dogs and spreads rapidly from one dog to another. Occasionally a vaccinated dog also contacts the disease. Symptoms include some or all of the following: diarrhea, vomiting, reduced appetite, cough, nasal discharge, inflamed eyes, fever, exhaustion and lack of interest in toys or games. While distemper victims are usually puppies, older dogs may contract it too. Dogs that receive immediate treatment have a better chance of survival, so if you ever suspect that your Irish Setter has distemper, take him to the veterinarian right away.

Infectious hepatitis in dogs is not transmissible to man, although it affects the liver just as it does in the human form. Caused by canine adenovirus type I, the disease spreads through contact with an infected dog's stool, urine or saliva. Intense thirst is one indication, but other symptoms are similar to those of distemper. The disease progresses rapidly and is often fatal, so prompt veterinary treatment is critical.

Leptospirosis is caused by a microorganism that is often carried by rats. This bacteria can also be passed through the urine of an infected dog. Symptoms include bloody diarrhea and/or blood in the urine, fever, depression, red and congested eyes and mouth membranes, painful mouth ulcers, vomiting, pain when moving, increased thirst, loss of appetite, and a red hue or jaundiced appearance in the whites of the eyes. Since the dog's liver and kidneys can be permanently damaged, quick veterinary treatment is essential. Humans can also contact leptospirosis, so observe your

veterinarian's precautions if your Irish Setter contracts this disease.

Believed to be a strain of feline distemper that mutated, the deadly parvovirus was unknown in dogs until 1977. The virus attacks the bone marrow, stomach lining and lymph nodes, and in young puppies, the heart. Passed through contaminated stools, it spreads rapidly from dog to dog. Early symptoms often include loss of appetite and depression and the disease quickly progresses to diarrhea (sometimes bloody), vomiting and fever. Puppies with infected hearts (myocardial parvovirus) breathe with difficulty, may foam at the nose and mouth and often die within one or two days of contracting the disease. Those few that recover may develop chronic heart problems later. When adult Irish Setters contract parvovirus, reactions vary. Some become violently ill, and others just lose their appetite for a day or two before returning to normal.

Parainfluenza is one of the viruses that causes infectious canine tracheobronchitis, commonly known as kennel cough. Kennel cough is caused by several different viruses as well as the *Bordetella* bacteria, and is highly contagious from dog to dog. Symptoms are a frequent dry, hacking cough and sometimes a nasal discharge. Adult Irish Setters infected with kennel cough may not even miss a meal, but the disease can be dangerous to puppies. While recovering, they should be kept in a warm, humid room. Your veterinarian may prescribe antibiotics to prevent complications and medication to control coughing for infected Irish Setters of all ages. Dogs vaccinated against parainfluenza sometimes come down with it anyway, but usually have milder symptoms than unvaccinated dogs.

Lyme disease is transmitted to people and dogs by two types of ticks; the more prevalent deer tick and the western black-legged tick. Symptoms of Lyme disease include fatigue, lameness, loss of appetite, fever and swollen joints. If you live in an area where the deer tick is prevalent, keep your lawn well trimmed, take precautions to keep field mice from nesting in your home and avoid walking in the woods. After hunting with your Irish Setter, examine him well and spray him with a tick-killing insecticide recommended by your veterinarian. There is a vaccine against Lyme disease, but since Lyme was first diagnosed in dogs in 1984, the vaccine is still being perfected and is not 100% effective.

Rabies is a viral disease that is always fatal, and a dog with rabies is a danger to humans and

PHOTO BY ISABELLE FRANCAIS.

Puppies that spend a lot of time on grass (and most Irish Setters love working in the field) might be subject to external parasites such as fleas and ticks. Be aware of it.

other animals. A vaccine prevents this dreaded disease. Your veterinarian will give the rabies shot separately, not in combination with the other vaccines, and will tell you when your Irish Setter's rabies vaccination should be renewed.

The rabies virus can infect dogs that come in contact with other animals, domestic or wild, that already have the virus. Rabies attacks the nervous system, and is most often spread by infected saliva — usually from a bite. It may also be transmitted through cuts or scratches that come in contact with saliva from a rabid animal. An early sign of rabies is a change in disposition. A gentle dog may become aggressive or an aloof dog may become loving. Later, the dog's pupils may dilate and light may become painful. Soon the dog will want to be left alone and may have stomach pains and a fever. Advanced symptoms are twitching facial muscles, bared teeth, random biting and lack of coordination. Eventually the dog loses control of its facial muscles, resulting in an open mouth with the tongue hanging out. The dog may drool, paw at his mouth and cough before he finally slips into a coma and dies. All warm-blooded animals are susceptible to rabies, so anyone bitten by a dog (or any other animal) should see a doctor right away.

That was quite a list of gloom and doom, but happily all diseases mentioned are preventable. Just remember to keep Big Red's vaccinations current.

PARASITES

No matter how well you take care of your Irish Setter, he may still become infested with internal parasites such as roundworm, hookworm, whipworm and tapeworm, and external parasites such as fleas, ticks and ear mites.

The symptoms of worm infestation usually include one or more of the following: a generally unsound appearance, a rough, dry coat, dull eyes, weight loss despite an enormous appetite, coughing, vomiting, weakness, diarrhea, and sometimes, bloody stools. Some dogs show no symptoms at all until they are seriously anemic from a heavy infestation, while others lose their appetite entirely when even mildly infested with worms.

On the bright side, worms are easily controllable. Just have your veterinarian check your dog's stool at least twice a year and if medication is prescribed, give it exactly as instructed.

The hazardous heartworm is transmitted from dog to dog by mosquito bites, and eight months or more may go by from the time a dog is bitten until the worms mature. Treatment is dangerous, but ignoring the condition is even worse. Symptoms of heartworm include weight loss, exhaustion and a chronic cough, as the worms interfere with the action of the dog's heart. The good news is that heartworm is preventable. A well-cared-for Irish Setter won't get heartworm because he will receive the preventative medication prescribed by his veterinarian. Puppies should be started on a preventative program at a young age and tested annually. Adult dogs must test free of the worms before they can begin a preventative regimen because the medication may make them deathly ill if they are already infested with adult heartworms.

Ticks, fleas and ear mites may all try to set up housekeeping on your Irish Setter. Ticks come in a

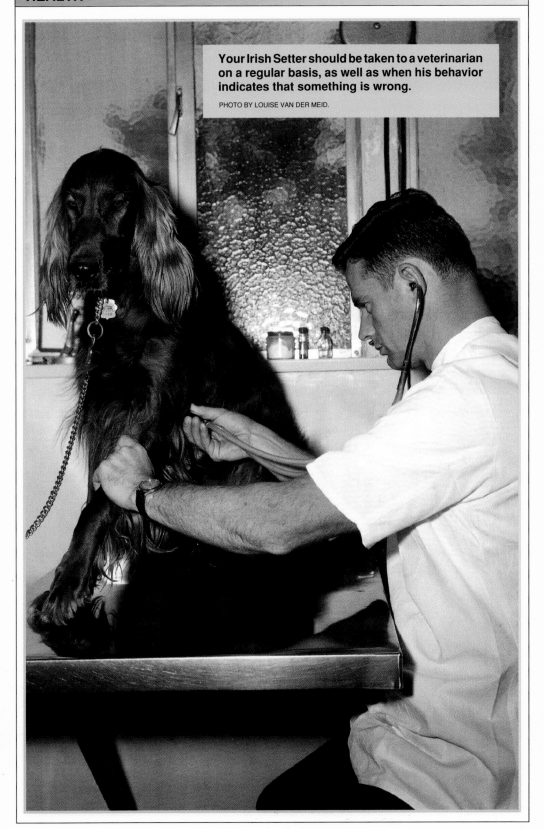

Your Irish Setter should be taken to a veterinarian on a regular basis, as well as when his behavior indicates that something is wrong.

PHOTO BY LOUISE VAN DER MEID.

variety of sizes and colors and seem to prefer the head and neck area, but may be found anywhere on the body. Your veterinarian will recommend a preparation that removes them safely and effectively. If you find a tick on your Irish Setter when you are far away from your medicine chest, separate your dog's hair so you can see where the tick embedded itself in the skin. The embedded part is its head. Using tweezers, clamp down as close to the head as possible and pull it out. If part of the head remains under your dog's skin, apply an antiseptic.

Fleas are very difficult to get rid of. New and updated versions of flea sprays, dips and powders appear on the market every year because fleas quickly become resistant to insecticides. Your veterinarian knows which preparations work best in your locale, so if your dog or your home is bothered by fleas, seek professional help. It's important to follow your veterinarian's instructions to the letter. Don't experiment with more than one flea remedy at the same time. A perfectly safe insecticide may become lethal when mixed with another insecticide.

Ear mites live in the ear canal, making your Irish Setter's sensitive ears sore and itchy, and producing a dry, rusty-brown discharge. This condition responds quickly to veterinary treatment.

CLOGGED ANAL GLANDS

If your Irish Setter scoots along the floor on his haunches, he probably has clogged anal glands. The anal glands, located on each side of the anus, secrete a substance that helps your dog pass his stool. They are extremely uncomfortable when clogged, smell bad and could easily become infected. Your veterinarian can easily unclog your Irish Setter's anal glands, or you can save yourself the trip and do it yourself. Use one hand to keep your dog's tail up and hold a soft tissue in your other hand. Take the skin on either side of the anus, just below the middle, in your thumb and forefinger. Push in slightly and squeeze gently. Soon a brownish, nasty smelling substance will stain your tissue, and your dog will stop scooting. Blood or pus in the secretion is a sign of infection, so, if either one is present, take your dog to the veterinarian.

SPAYING AND NEUTERING

The nicest thing you can do for yourself and your Irish Setter is to have your dog spayed or neutered. Females spayed before their first season are at much less risk of developing breast cancer than unspayed females, and they never develop cancers or infections of the ovaries or uterus since they have no reproductive organs. They are also easier to live with as they don't bleed all over your house for several days twice a year, or develop an urge to roam, or entice males to your door, or have unwanted, expensive and often dangerous pregnancies.

Neutering a male dog has its pluses too. It often makes him

PHOTO BY ISABELLE FRANCAIS.

Spaying/neutering is often the best option for your family pet. The health benefits are numerous and it will minimize the risk of certain diseases.

easier to housebreak and stabilizes his disposition. Having the operation performed before he is a year old could also save him the pain of prosrate problems, including cancer, when he ages.

Don't believe the old wives' tale that spaying or neutering makes a dog fat and lazy. Over-feeding and lack of exercise do that. The fact is that spayed and neutered pets have better concentration and are often the top performers in obedience, agility and other competitive sports. Spayed and neutered dogs are welcome in obedience and agility competition and hunting tests, but since dog shows are a showcase for breeding stock, altered animals are not permitted to compete in conformation. If a show career is in your puppy's future, refrain from spaying or neutering until your dog retires from competition.

EXERCISE

The smooth muscles beneath your Irish Setter's sleek coat are not the only muscles that are toned and conditioned by regular exercise. His heart is made of muscle and even his intestines contain muscle tissue. Blood supply to the muscles is dependent on regular exercise. That means your Irishman will live longer and be more attractive if he has sufficient exercise. He will also be better behaved. Many behavior problems in dogs, especially in active sporting breeds like Irish Setters, can be traced to lack of exercise. Big Red needs a good workout every day.

There are many ways to exercise your Irish Setter. Brisk walks are terrific for both of you, but, unless you are training for a marathon, your dog may require additional exercise. He'll be able to make his workout a do-it-yourself project if provided with a securely fenced yard. Make sure your dog's play area has sufficient shade, fresh water and a couple of his favorite toys. If he spends time in the yard while you are away, he will also need protection from the elements. As ably as Irish Setters exercise themselves, your dog will be even happier if you or the children play games with him. Teach him to play ball or Frisbee and you'll be able to give Big Red plenty of exercise, even while sitting or standing in place. Dogs can also take part in many

Exercise is an absolute necessity for your dog and is important for your health as well. Brisk walking is ideal for both of you.

PHOTO BY VINCE SERBIN.

The ideal exercise/training is retrieval. There is only one Frisbee®* made especially for dogs and that's the Gumabone® Frisbee®* with the dog bone molded on top of it. This Frisbee®* is scented and made of extremely strong nylon. Don't accept substitutes or your Irishman might tear up the cheap plastic and swallow it! * The trademark Frisbee is used under license from Mattel, Inc. California, USA.

children's games, such as keep-away, hide-and-seek and tag, and sometimes even seem to understand the object of these games.

Best of all, there are a myriad of activities especially for dogs, and Big Red is eminently suited to excel in many of them. To become a good companion, he should attend a novice obedience or agility class anyway, so why not turn his training into a hobby that's fun for both of you? Preparing for either activity is good exercise, besides adding purpose and pride to your dog's life. In addition, the Irish Setter is eligible for hunting tests (you don't have to be a hunter to participate), and both of you can learn all about this sport through your local hunting test club. To find an obedience, agility or hunting test club near you, contact the American Kennel Club (AKC), 5580 Centerview Dr., Suite 200, Raleigh, North Carolina 27606, (919) 233-9780 or the United Kennel Club (UKC), 100 East Kilgore Rd., Kalamazoo, Michigan 49001, (616) 343-9020 or the Canadian Kennel Club, 111 Elington Avenue, East Ontario, Ontario M6S4VT, Canada.

GROOMING YOUR IRISH SETTER

Daily care will keep your Irish Setter's brilliant coat clean and shiny, but the rewards go way beyond that. Grooming your dog's silky coat just plain feels good — to you and your dog — and pleasant, relaxing grooming sessions strengthen the bond between dog and owner. Regular coat care also saves money. While you are grooming, inspect your dog for minor injuries, early signs of skin disease and external parasites. Solving problems when they are small keeps them from turning into big, expensive complications.

Grooming your gorgeous Irish Setter could become one of your favorite pastimes. The trick is to start early and introduce your puppy to the process patiently. If you condition your Irish Setter from puppyhood to accept grooming as a regular part of life, he will soon enjoy your touch, look forward to the attention and cooperate by holding still. But if you wait until he is a mess of mats and then try to rush the job, your hasty detangling methods will hurt him and he will wiggle and struggle. Worst of all, he will remember grooming as a painful experience, and as he grows larger, he will struggle all the harder. Eventually he may learn to trust you when you have a brush or toenail clipper in your hand, but nothing saves more time in the long run than a slow, patient start.

Introduce your Irish Setter puppy to the grooming procedure by gently but firmly placing him on the grooming table (or on the floor in the part of the house where you will be grooming if you don't plan to use a table). Praise him just for being there and let him sniff around a little if he is so inclined. Then just stroke him for a minute or two from head to tail and from brisket to belly, talking softly to him the entire time. Lift each foot and put it down, lift each ear and look inside and run your hand down his tail from base to tip. If a professionally finished look is what you want, your puppy will have to get used to the sound and vibration of the electric clippers and hair dryer. Don't get those noisy implements too close to his ears during the introduction, but do let him hear them run by holding each one in one hand while petting him with the other hand. The entire introduction to grooming should take no longer than five minutes. Finish by giving your puppy a treat while he is still on the table (or in the grooming area), then hug him close to you and set him gently down on the floor. Repeat this brief process at least three times on three different days before you even touch your Irish Setter with a brush.

The first time you actually groom your Irish Setter puppy, use only your hands and your natural bristle brush. Talk to your

The main physical attraction of an Irish Setter is his beautiful red coat. This requires daily brushing to remove dead hairs and invigorate the skin to produce natural oils that make the coat shiny.

PHOTO BY ISABELLE FRANCAIS.

puppy softly while you work, but if he becomes fidgety about being handled on any part of his body, say "no" sharply and firmly and continue grooming. Soon your dog will learn that grooming sessions are a mixture of fun and work. Fun, because all that attention is great and being brushed feels wonderful. Work, because he is expected to behave. By the time your Irish Setter is half grown, he should be relaxed and cooperative during grooming sessions.

You can groom your Irish Setter on the floor, but a grooming table may be easier on your back. Standing on a table also makes many dogs more cooperative. Grooming tables must be sturdy, have a non-slip surface such as ribbed rubber matting and stand square, without a hint of wobble. You can make one yourself or buy one at a dog show booth or through a pet supply catalog. They are available in a variety of sizes and the largest is just right for an Irish Setter. If you are on the short side, you may want to have the table legs cut down a couple inches after your puppy grows up. That will make it easier for you to reach his head. Grooming tables usually have folding legs so they are easy to move from one location to another or to store when not in use. Some of them come with an adjustable arm and a loop that fits around the dog's neck to help keep him steady. Never leave your Irish Setter alone on the table or even turn your back on him (even if the loop is around his neck). It takes less than an instant for a dog to jump or fall, and the results can be tragic.

COAT AND SKIN CARE

Daily brushing with a natural bristle brush will keep your Irish Setter's skin and coat healthy and shiny. Brushing removes dirt, dead hair, loose skin particles and dandruff, while stimulating circulation and the secretion of natural skin oils. Be sure to concentrate on your Irish Setter's flowing feathers, which should receive finishing touches with a metal comb to remove loose hair and tiny tangles. While brushing your dog, check for minor injuries, ticks and fleas. Although you may find a tick attached to any part of your dog, they often hide between the toes, in the ears, in the neck area, just in front of the tail and in the areas where your dog's hair is thickest. To find fleas, rough your dog's coat in the opposite direction from the way it grows. Tiny black specks on the skin are a sign that fleas are present, even if you don't actually see a flea. Ask your veterinarian to recommend an insecticide shampoo or dip and a product to rid your home of fleas, and always use these preparations exactly as recommended on the label.

Regular grooming keeps mats to a minimum but an occasional mat will still find its way behind your dog's ears, under his armpits or beneath his attractive feathers. Instead of pulling, take the pain out of dematting by using a detangler solution. Soak the mat all the way to the skin and then try to work it out with your fingers. Pin brushes and slicker brushes also aid in removing mats from the ears, chest, legs and tail, but may hurt a dog with extremely sensitive skin if used in the armpit area. If your attempt to remove a mat fails or hurts your dog, use a scissors with a rounded tip and cut the mat away close to the skin.

To groom your dog's tail, hold it by the tip so it is straight out from the body and comb the feathering downward with your metal dog comb. If the hair has become too long to be neat and attractive, use a quality scissors to trim it. Tail feathering should be longest at the base (near the body) and taper to a point at the tip.

Your scissors and metal comb can also be used to make your dog's feet neat and tidy. Comb the hair between your dog's toes upward and trim it flush with the top of the foot. Then scissor away any straggly hair around or on top of your dog's feet.

If you want your Irish Setter to sport a more professionally finished appearance, you'll have to learn to clip and trim him. Buy a good quality clipper and a #10 and a #7 blade to go with it, along with quality scissors and thinning shears. Invest in a professional grooming for your dog before trying to do it yourself, and make arrangements beforehand to

You and your Irish Setter can enjoy hours of fun with a Nylafloss®. It does wonders for your dog's dental health by massaging his gums and literally flossing between his teeth, loosening plaque and tartar build-up. Unlike cotton tug toys, Nylafloss® is made of 100% virgin nylon and won't rot or fray.

watch the process. If you decide to leave the finishing touches to a professional, continue your daily grooming, but take your dog to the salon approximately every two months.

SHOW GROOMING

Are you planning a show career for your dog? Then do your daily grooming, but stop short of touching your dog with scissors, clippers or thinning shears until your dog's breeder or a respected professional handler has taught you the intricate details of keeping an Irish Setter's coat in competitive condition.

TOENAILS AND TEETH

Your Irish Setter's toenails are too long if they touch the ground when he is standing still or make clicking noises on the floor when he walks. This is uncomfortable and can lead to splayed toes and an unattractive gait. Toenail trimmers in a variety of styles are available at most pet supply stores. The heavy duty plier type (a blade at both ends) works best on an Irish Setter.

To clip your Irishman's nails, lift his foot up and forward. Then hold it firmly in your left hand so your right hand can do the trimming (reverse this if you are left-handed). When you cut the nail properly, your dog will feel nothing more than slight pressure, the same as you feel when cutting your own toenails. But if you accidentally cut the quick, the vein running through each nail, his nail will hurt and

As a pet owner, it is essential to keep your dog's teeth clean by removing surface tartar and plaque. 2-Brush™ by Nylabone® is made with two toothbrushes to clean both sides of your dog's teeth at the same time. Each brush contains a reservoir designed to apply the toothpaste, which is specially formulated for dogs, directly into the toothbrush.

bleed and he may become leery of having his toenails trimmed. If you can see the pink quick through your dog's nails it's easy to avoid cutting it, but most Irish Setters have toenails too dark to see through. In that case, make the cut just outside the hook-like projection on the underside of the nail. Work under good lighting so you can cut your dog's nails without a mishap, but if you accidentally cut the quick (everybody makes an occasional mistake), stop the bleeding with a styptic pencil made for human use or use the styptic powder sold at pet supply stores. Pressing the bleeding nail into a soft bar of soap for a minute or so will also stop the bleeding.

To check your Irish Setter's teeth for tartar, hold his head steady and gently push his lips upward. If there are discolorations, use a soft baby toothbrush or the end of a damp washcloth dipped in baking soda. Check with your veterinarian if the stains won't budge. Your dog's teeth may need a professional cleaning.

BATHING

Your Irish Setter will seldom need a bath if he is brushed briefly every day. Shampooing washes away the natural oils that moisturize the coat and skin, so bathe your dog only when necessary.

Equipment for a bath includes: old clothes (when Big Red shakes, you'll get mighty wet); a tub, preferably with a drain so your dog won't have to stand in soapy water; a rubber mat for traction in the tub; a spray-nozzle hose attachment or an unbreakable cup for dipping water; pH-balanced dog shampoo (or insecticide shampoo or dip if necessary); cotton balls; a washcloth or two; mineral oil; and a couple of heavy towels. Coat conditioner following the shampoo and a blow dryer are optional.

Walk your Irish Setter or put him outside for a few minutes before beginning the bath.

Otherwise he may want to rush outdoors to relieve himself (and roll in the grass or loose garden dirt) immediately following the bath. Then give him a brief brushing, making sure he is free of mats before bathing him.

Start by placing a cotton ball inside each of your Irish Setter's ears to keep the water out. Next, spray or pour water (warm, but not hot) over your dog's whole body with the exception of his face and head. Put a small amount of shampoo on his back and massage the lather into his coat. (If you are using insecticide shampoo or dip, follow the label directions carefully). Add more shampoo as needed and work the lather into his neck, chest, legs, underbelly and tail. If your Irish Setter has profuse feathering, a washcloth will be helpful in working the suds all the way to the skin. Take care to avoid getting soap in your dog's eyes, but if some suds accidentally splash into an eye, relieve the sting by placing a few drops of mineral oil in the inner corner of the eye. When your Irish Setter is clean, thoroughly rinse off the lather. Never rush — this most important step. When shampoo dries in the coat it can cause intense itching and dull the shine.

Wipe your dog's face and head with a warm, well-wrung washcloth. Then remove the cotton from his ears and clean each ear gently with a dry cotton ball dipped in a tiny bit of mineral oil. Finish by towel-drying your dog well, blotting the heavily feathered areas and paying special attention to his chest and underbelly. If your dog has especially long or thick feathering, fluff him dry with a blow dryer. By the time he is dried and brushed, your active Irishman will be more than ready to go for a walk and show off his gleaming coat. But he'll have to wait a bit. Keep your bundle of energy indoors until he is dry all the way to the skin and then walk him on lead until his inclination to roll in the dirt has passed.

This Gumabone® Tug Toy is made from non-slippery material which enables your Irish Setter to be exercised while he is having his gums massaged.

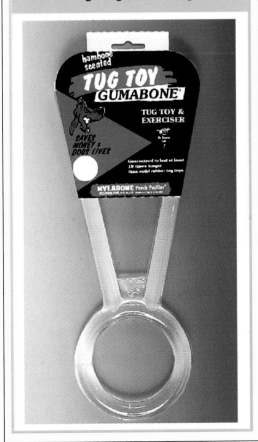

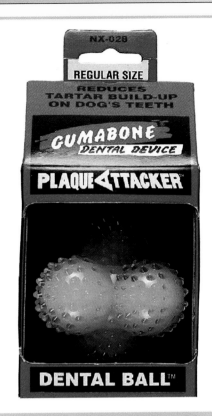

The Plaque-Attacker™ Dental Ball™ is the accepted standard for exercise and good dental care. The spikes break up the growth of plaque. All products recommended in this book are available at your local pet shop.

MORE THAN SKIN DEEP

While good grooming practices will enhance your Irish Setter's natural good looks, it won't disguise ill health or poor muscle tone. In fact, sometimes the first sign of a health problem is a dry, lackluster coat. Clean housing, quality food and no internal or external parasites all contribute to Big Red's beauty. Healthy Irish Setters sparkle from the inside out. Their regular grooming sessions help them stay in top form and bring the wholesome glow to the surface.

FEEDING

Now let's talk about feeding your Irish Setter, a subject so simple that it's amazing there is so much nonsense and misunderstanding about it. Is it expensive to feed a Irish Setter? No, it is not! You can feed your Irish Setter economically and keep him in perfect shape the year round, or you can feed him expensively. He'll thrive either way, and let's see why this is true.

First of all, remember a Irish Setter is a dog. Dogs do not have a high degree of selectivity in their food, and unless you spoil them with great variety (and possibly turn them into poor, "picky" eaters) they will eat almost anything that they become accustomed to. Many dogs flatly refuse to eat nice, fresh beef. They pick around it and eat everything else. But meat—bah! Why? They aren't accustomed to it! They'd eat rabbit fast enough, but they refuse beef because they aren't used to it.

VARIETY NOT NECESSARY

A good general rule of thumb is forget all human preferences and don't give a thought to variety. Choose the right diet for your Irish Setter and feed it to him day after day, year after year, winter and summer. But what is the right diet?

Hundreds of thousands of dollars have been spent in canine

One of the few health bones for dogs. The Carrot Bone is the only all-vegetable bone made with carrots. It's very hard and your Irish Setter will enjoy it as a chew device. If it is too hard, simply bake it or microwave it (30-60 seconds) and it will become much softer.

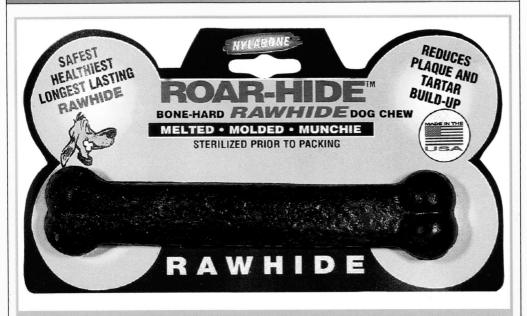

Roar-Hide™ is a completely edible product that is high in protein (over 86%) and low in fat (less than one-third of 1%). Unlike common rawhide, it is safer, less messy, and more fun for your Irish Setter.

nutrition research. The results are pretty conclusive, so you needn't go into a lot of experimenting with trials of this and that every other week. Research has proven just what your dog needs to eat and to keep healthy.

DOG FOOD

There are almost as many right diets as there are dog experts, but the basic diet most often recommended is one that consists of a dry food, either meal or kibble form. There are several of excellent quality, manufactured by reliable companies, research tested, and nationally advertised. They are inexpensive, highly satisfactory, and easily available in stores everywhere in containers of five to 50 pounds. Larger amounts cost less per pound, usually.

If you have a choice of brands, it is usually safer to choose the better known one; but even so, carefully read the analysis on the package. Do not choose any food in which the protein level is less than 25 percent, and be sure that this protein comes from both animal and vegetable sources. The good dog foods have meat meal, fish meal, liver, and such, plus protein from alfalfa and soy beans, as well as some dried-milk product. Note the vitamin content carefully. See that they are all there in good proportions; and be especially certain that the food contains properly high levels of vitamins A and D, two of the most perishable and important ones. Note the B-complex level, but don't worry about carbohydrate and mineral levels. These substances are plentiful and cheap and not likely to be lacking in a good brand.

The advice given for how to choose a dry food also applies to moist or canned types of dog foods, if you decide to feed one of these.

Having chosen a really good food, feed it to your Irish Setter as the manufacturer directs. And once you've started, stick to it. Never change if you can possibly help it. A switch from one meal or kibble-type food can usually be made without too much upset; however, a change will almost invariably give you (and your Irish Setter) some trouble.

WHEN SUPPLEMENTS ARE NEEDED

Now what about supplements of various kinds, mineral and vitamin, or the various oils? They are all okay to add to your Irish Setter's food. However, if you are feeding your Irish Setter a correct diet, and this is easy to do, no supplements are necessary unless your Irish Setter has been improperly fed, has been sick, or is having puppies. Vitamins and minerals are naturally present in all the foods; and to ensure against any loss through processing, they are added in concentrated form to the dog food you use. Except on the advice of your veterinarian, added amounts of vitamins can prove harmful to your Irish Setter! The same risk goes with minerals.

FEEDING SCHEDULE

When and how much food to give your Irish Setter? Most dogs do better if fed two or three smaller meals per day—this is not only better but vital to larger and deep-chested dogs. As to how to prepare the food and how much to give, it is generally best to follow the directions on the food package. Your own Irish Setter may want a little more or a little less.

Fresh, cool water should always be available to your Irish Setter. This is important to good health throughout his lifetime.

ALL IRISH SETTERS NEED TO CHEW

Puppies and young Irish Setters need something with resistance to chew on while their teeth and jaws are developing—for cutting the puppy teeth, to induce growth of the permanent teeth under the puppy teeth, to assist in getting rid of the puppy teeth at the proper time, to help the permanent teeth through the gums, to ensure normal jaw development, and to settle the permanent teeth solidly in the jaws.

The adult Irish Setter's desire to chew stems from the instinct for tooth cleaning, gum massage, and jaw exercise—plus the need for an outlet for periodic doggie tensions.

This is why dogs, especially puppies and young dogs, will often destroy property worth hundreds of dollars when their chewing instinct is not diverted from their owner's possessions. And this is why you should provide your Irish Setter with something to chew—something that has the necessary functional qualities, is desirable from the Irish Setter's viewpoint, and is safe for him.

It is very important that your Irish Setter not be permitted to chew on anything he can break or on any indigestible thing from which he can bite sizable chunks. Sharp pieces, such as from a bone which can be broken by a dog, may pierce the intestinal wall and kill. Indigestible things that can be bitten off in chunks, such as from shoes or rubber or plastic toys, may cause an intestinal stoppage (if not regurgitated) and bring painful death, unless surgery is promptly performed.

Strong natural bones, such as 4- to 8-inch lengths of round shin bone from mature beef—either the kind you can get from a butcher or one of the variety available commercially in pet stores—may serve your Irish Setter's teething needs if his mouth is large enough to handle them effectively. You may be tempted to give your Irish Setter puppy a smaller bone and he may not be able to break it when you do, but puppies grow rapidly and the power of their jaws constantly increases until maturity. This means that a growing Irish Setter may break one of the smaller bones at any time, swallow the pieces, and die painfully before you realize what is wrong.

All hard natural bones are very abrasive. If your Irish Setter is an avid chewer, natural bones may wear away his teeth prematurely; hence, they then should be taken away from your dog when the teething purposes have been served. The badly worn, and usually painful, teeth of many mature dogs can be traced to excessive chewing on natural bones.

Contrary to popular belief, knuckle bones that can be chewed up and swallowed by your Irish Setter provide little, if any, usable calcium or other nutriment. They do, however, disturb the digestion of most dogs and cause them to vomit the nourishing food they need.

Dried rawhide products of various types, shapes, sizes, and prices are available on the market and have become quite popular. However, they don't serve the primary chewing functions very well; they are a bit messy when wet from mouthing, and most Irish Setters chew them up rather rapidly—but they have been considered safe for dogs until recently. Now, more and more incidents of death, and near death, by strangulation have been reported to be the results of partially swallowed chunks of rawhide swelling in the throat. More recently, some veterinarians have been attributing cases of acute constipation to large pieces of incompletely digested rawhide in the intestine.

A new product, molded rawhide, is very safe. During the process, the rawhide is melted and then injection molded into the familiar dog shape. It is very hard and is eagerly accepted by Irish Setters. The melting process also sterilizes the rawhide. Don't confuse this with pressed rawhide, which is nothing more than small strips of rawhide squeezed together.

The nylon bones, especially those with natural meat and bone fractions added, are probably the most complete, safe, and economical answer to the chewing need. Dogs cannot break them or bite off sizable chunks; hence, they are completely safe—and being longer lasting than other things offered for the purpose, they are economical.

Hard chewing raises little bristle-like projections on the surface of the nylon bones—to provide effective interim tooth cleaning and vigorous gum massage, much in the same way your toothbrush does it for you. The little projections are raked off and swallowed in the form of thin shavings, but the chemistry of the nylon is such that they break down in the stomach fluids and pass through without effect.

The toughness of the nylon provides the strong chewing resistance needed for important jaw exercise and effectively aids teething functions, but there is no tooth wear because nylon is non-abrasive. Being inert, nylon does not support the growth of microorganisms; and it can be washed in soap and water or it can be sterilized by boiling or in an autoclave.

Nylabone® is highly recommended by veterinarians as a safe, healthy nylon bone that can't splinter or chip. Nylabone® is frizzled by the dog's chewing action, creating a toothbrush-like surface that cleanses the teeth and massages the gums. Nylabone®, the only chew products made of flavor-impregnated solid nylon, are available in your local pet shop. Nylabone® is superior to the cheaper bones because it is made of virgin nylon, which is the strongest and longest-lasting type of nylon available. The cheaper bones are made from recycled or re-ground nylon scraps, and have a tendency to break apart and split easily.

Nothing, however, substitutes for periodic professional attention for your Irish Setter's teeth and gums, not any more than your toothbrush can do that for you. Have your Irish Setter's teeth cleaned at least once a year by your veterinarian (twice a year is better) and he will be happier, healthier, and far more pleasant to live with.

Nylabones® are the only plastic bones recommended by veterinarians and accepted for advertising in the *Journal of the American Veterinary Association.* Simply put, it's the best for Irish Setters as well as other large dogs with strong teeth and jaws.